The essence of cruising

The essence of cruising

Des Sleightholme

fernhurst
B O O K S

www.fernhurstbooks.co.uk

© Fernhurst Books 2001

First published 2001 by
Fernhurst Books,
Duke's Path, High Street, Arundel,
West Sussex, BN18 9AJ, England.

British Library Cataloguing in Publication Data.
A catalogue record for this book is available from the
British Library.

ISBN 1 898660 84 0

Printed in China through World Print
Artwork by Creative Byte

Cover design by Simon Balley
Cover photos by Rick Tomlinson and Tim Davison

CONTENTS

1. First boats and first steps

A first boat is like a girl's first boyfriend
- later she'll wonder what the hell she saw in him!
It's not a bad idea to buy a second-hand,
popular class of yacht which can be traded in
without financial loss in a year or so,
once you know what you really want.

The price of the boat may be about half the total cost of going sailing.
Better a smaller boat properly equipped.
Resist boat show phobia, the 'Aw heck,
what's another thousand!' syndrome.

The smaller the crew the more you'll sail her.
Accommodation for ten, great!
You'll spend your time ringing round your
friends every time you want to go sailing.
A boat big enough for sea-going with
a couple of mates is a better bet.

A family that sails together stays together.
Provided you start
when kids are small.
If you buy a boat and expect
them to give up pony riding
at weekends you're on
a hiding to nowhere!

Cruising under sail?
Buy an alarm clock and cancel everything else.
Early calls and dawn tides, ghosting around
headlands are a challenge to some, boring to others.
Then forget it and buy a fifty-fifty.

Don't buy a Stradivarius and strum it like a ukulele.
Or a smart sailer and motor every time
the wind fades or comes ahead.

In a crew of novices, the one
who knows most is Admiral.

Provided it doesn't inflate the ego and lead to over-ambitious
plans, a novice crew learning as they go will guarantee
a lot of laughter, good-fellowship and mud all-round.

Buy a nautical Wendy-house, forget the world cruise.

A plump little boat that sails like a garden shed can
be regarded as a weekend chalet and sailed gently
from creek-to-creek. Nothing wrong with that
- especially if it woos a nervous partner.

Nobody ever wrecked a blackboard.
We may learn the theory in a warm,
dry classroom but we can't heel it thirty degrees and
blast salt spray through it – so the reality may be a shock.
The aim is to remember what's vital.

The sea makes no concessions.
We treat it as a playground at our peril:
professional sailor or amateur,
it blows the same gales and demands
the same skills of one and all.

**Reading avidly is like
hoarding – some day that
stuffed badger
may come in handy.**
When the custard hits the fan,
something once read
and lying buried in the
subconscious can
come back to you.
Knowing what to do
is half way to
being able to do it.

2. The skipper's job

Think twice, order once.

A tense situation can lead to a skipper rapping out
orders and then countermanding them. Result, chaos.
Don't shout except to be heard above wind and water.
Cool skipper, cool crew.

Flat batteries, feeble light.

Don't start a passage with a tired crew longing for kip;
seasickness and resentment follow. You may take a daft
risk making for shelter unwisely.
Be late for work rather than risk your necks.

Don't tack faster than the crew can move.
If you have a racing crew then fine, ship her around
– otherwise give them time to sheet home comfortably.
Would-be Olympic helmsman versus mother and
cousin Blanche are a recipe for domestic disaster.

Where there's wind there's water.
Drive a boat hard and you get wet.
The cruising philosophy allows us to crack
sheets a little and take it a bit easier
- a longer passage maybe, but more enjoyable.

Weekend sailor and Master-under-God.

It is a dangerous temptation for men
to get drunk on authority!
They cannot fool their wives who know
them as little men in their shirt-tails.
The best cure is for them to crew in
a crack yacht under a real skipper.

Look at the clouds and listen to the halyards
First job of the day, then check barometer and forecast.
In a marina you can't assess the wind speed.
Forecasted weather may not have arrived
- or it may have passed. Fast-moving upper cloud
may warn of a wind due to strengthen.

**There's a lot to see in the hedgerow
that you miss by staring at the hills.**
Learn your home waters first, that way you'll all be
relaxed and in control and there's more than enough
to make your hair stand on end near at home.
Tackle the long haul next season.

Look-outs are only as good as their eyes.
Crew can be myopic, colour-blind or have
other undisclosed problems with their eyes.
A diplomatic skipper finds out - also teaches novices
what to look for and what distant marks will look like.

One ship one captain.
Other skippers may decide to go to sea; that's their
decision based upon their skills and their crew.
Take a long look at your own and then decide for yourself.

Mow the lawn or scrub the bottom?
Unless married partners are united in their passion for sailing,
the home-job-or-boat-job issue can become
a threat to harmony and boat ownership.
Many a sailing - and married - relationship
founders on this knobbly rock.

Big worry or small problem?
The difference may be an empty belly. When cold, wet
and hungry you become demoralised and pessimistic.
Crew morale is as tangible a factor as shortage of fuel
and headwinds. Once crew stop being rude to each
other you've got trouble.

**A yelling skipper alienates
the crew and entertains
the neighbours.**
Save yells for the emergency
that needs a shot of adrenalin
- indignant crew
heave harder.
Otherwise orders should
be given clearly but quietly
with the bellow held in reserve.

Knowing your position is fine - but knowing where you were can be important to knowing where you will be.

Blind reliance on electronics is unwise.

Use every possible form of confirmation.

Keep a well-written log - it may also be essential
evidence in a legal dispute.

A passage-plan is to use - don't let it use you.

It's real value is that it makes you do the thinking in advance,
study charts and note the options and alternatives.

Don't end up blatting along at full throttle
just to keep to the plan.

You might as well be catching the 8.25.

In a crisis the skipper decides and acts.
The crew must not expect to be consulted
when the tanker is bearing down.
Committees are democratic but
a politically correct skipper can kill you!

Wake me if you're worried.
The only way a skipper can get his head down
with confidence is in the knowledge that he/she
will be called by the crew when they're worried or uncertain.
If it's because the loo won't flush,
give a death's head grin and bear it!

Safe decisions may also be sour ones.
A good skipper accepts being a pain in the butt at times,
if the good of the ship is at stake.
What's an extra night at sea rather than
being squared up alongside a friendly bar!

No boat is any better than her crew allows her to be.
And if her crew consists of charming friends who are
useless in a boat, then anchor in some nice spot,
enjoy their company and a good bottle of wine.
Don't strain a relationship by revealing their inadequacy.

The cap doesn't make the captain.
Never 'pretend',
real sailors will see through you and the sea is unforgiving.

3. Crews and crewing

Different ships, different long-splices.
Skippers do things differently from boat to boat
- they hate being told how superior old so-and-so's
method in such-and-such boat may be.
Do it his way and learn something new.

Any fool can blow a flute or steer a boat.
It doesn't make you a flautist or a helmsman.
It takes years and a great deal of humility.

**Pick up a coil of rope and I'll tell you
whether you're novice or seaman.**
A seaman automatically re-coils it,
capsizes the coil on deck or hangs it by its cleat,
a novice doesn't even notice it or walks on it.

Sailor scanning for a buoy or nosey neighbour
- both favour the sidelong stare.
Peripheral vision, although a narrower band, is keener than
a frontal stare. The trick is to scan lazily and slowly, alert for
that tell-tale flicker (and I'm not one to gossip, as you know!).

It's easy to hate a fellow crew with porridge in his beard.
With a long-distance cruise in prospect, an initial short
cruise for people to get acquainted makes good sense.
Gibraltar is as far as many cruises get. Try Cornflakes.

Head warm and 'ass dry (fisherman's saying).

There is massive body heat loss via the scalp;
wear a warm waterproof hat.
A wet bum is demoralising and (sic) leads to piles!

Soft pillow, safer ship.

Sailors can sleep almost anywhere and through
almost anything provided the head is comfortable
- which it is not with a pillow made
of wellies wrapped in a sweater.
Comfortable, contained bunks are essential.

Captain Bligh in khaki knickers.
And the crews' perennial pain is a pompous skipper.
Quote something he won't know like the regulation lights
for taxiing seaplanes. Catch him out talking bull.

Bad crew walk straight past the unwashed mugs.
Good ones, used to living and sharing in small boats,
wash them up without a thought.
Brownie points and the sort of guy for a tight spot.

Crew on deck, ease her, slow her.
Not in racers, but crew working forr'd in a cruiser
are under the helmsman's scrutiny.
Nurse her along.
Take an extra turn with the mainsheet
if crew are hanging on to the boom.

Steer to a star.
Which means one eye on the compass.
On a dark night it becomes hypnotic; steering with the mast
against a star allows you to make an easy, swinging course.
Remember though, stars move across the heavens.

If a rope has to run, flake it don't coil it.

Halyard, kedge rope or any line that must run free and
unattended - lay criss-crossed on the deck
or in a bucket. As long as it
is left undisturbed it will run
without a hitch.

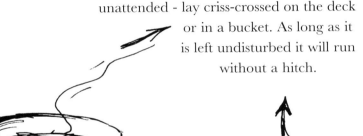

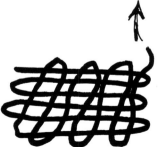

There are no decimal places in snap headings.

'Quick, what shall I steer ?'

pipes the helmsman in panic.

A novice navigator, hot from night-class,

works out Dev and Var plus tidal set

and the cat's birthday.

'Nor east' barks the veteran

and then works it out.

Hard to get in, harder to get out.

It's easy to ram bulky dinghies etc down forehatches, harder to get them out. Rig a whip tackle from the mast. Cockpit lockers are a greater problem: try a parbuckle strop.

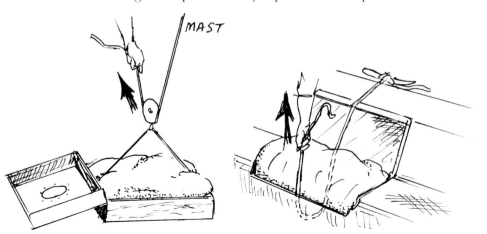

'I turned the gas off dear.'
'Did you dear? So did I.'
A 'leaving-the-boat' routine is vital
to ensure that gas, seacocks, log impeller, burgee
and so on are dealt with, but it's a job for one person!
Guess who has to drive
all the way back to check.

Go on watch five minutes early.

You not only spread joy and happiness but you clear
your head and get your night vision if it's a night watch.
Have a look at the chart as you pass
and get the off-going crowd to brief you;
e.g. course, lie of land, shipping.

**Your hands should make knots and hitches,
not your brain.**

You shouldn't have to think
how to make a bowline (for instance).
Learn half a dozen useful bends and hitches
which you can tie, in the dark, without thinking,
in a gale, and with somebody bawling at you to hurry.

A well-crewed vessel is a silent one.

Crew work without orders,
everybody knows what has to be done.
Silent crews are experts
- or have the most shocking hangovers!

Any idiot can tack, it's gybing that matters.

If the skipper-navigator is the only person aboard who can take
the helm on a dead run, the ship is unsafe. In a crisis she may
have to be steered down a narrow rocky channel in the dark!
Learn to run and to gybe.

**A racer's cockpit is a great school
for cruising sailors.**
That's if they can win a place in it.
They will learn engine-less sailing in all
weathers and precise sail-trimming
- alas these are arts which many cruising yachtsmen
replace with the engine starter button.

Twenty-five seconds
to coil and five to throw.

With thirty seconds in which to heave
a line take time to coil it small and neatly
otherwise you'll need a second attempt.
Divide the coil, secure one end, give a
full-arm swing and let the coils trip off
your other open hand.

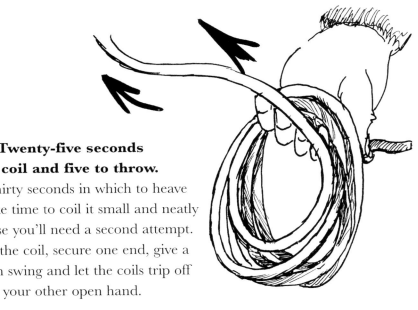

Nagged skippers make mistakes.
Don't niggle with petty gripes like
'they're going, why can't we?'

A slap-up meal but a sea-sick cook.
On short hops don't expect the cook to perform
gymnastics among the flying pans, save it for when you get in.
A cheese butty is worth 500 calories
- a grown man needs a daily 3,500.

Chocolate or cheese but never both.
A large hunk of cheese or a whole
bar of chocolate will keep you going but
DON'T combine them.
Many people suffer debilitating migraines!

Yawns and navigational sums don't mix.
Tired brains are suspect - we can make the most absurd mistakes.
Double-check your sums or better still get somebody else to do it
- that way you can shift the blame!

Don't go ape if you can't sleep.
People often get desperate if they can't sleep off-watch.
Just relax, dribble over a book, once you get really tired
and your body-clock catches up
you'll go out as if you'd been sand-bagged.

A sense of position
is more than a cross on the chart.
A spatial awareness is relating self with
chart and the layout of land and sea around you.
When going on watch get the watch on deck to brief you:
Lizard Head there, course this, tidal set that,
ship's heading so-and-so etc.

A back-bearing is better than an extra life-ring.
Man overboard! The reciprocal QUICK!
Add (or subtract) 180 degrees.

Bright sunlight tells lies at sea.
Buoys up-sun are like black specks, down-sun they show colour
and shape. Sun on a wet road looks like a white beacon,
deep shadow and bright sunlight alter shapes, hide or
emphasize marks. Use a pin-hole in a bit of cardboard
to exclude glitter or stare through a clenched fist.

Luff in a puff, sag in a lull.
To work a boat to windward ignore the compass,
follow the windshifts which means steering a sinuous course.
Many boats sail themselves better than cousin Percy,
sawing away at the helm.

Saggy luff and baggy leach, only good to run or reach.
Carelessly set sails may pass unnoticed down-wind but
on the wind she'll sail like a nun's bonnet.
At every dominant change of course check halyard
tension and sheeting angles.

An offshore wind is a sneaky one.
Sunshine and sparkle, but a mile offshore you may
be knocked flat. Reef early and adequately to avoid
a struggle to get back to shelter.

The time to reef is when you first think about it.
The longer you delay the harder it becomes.
When on the wind it's easier to judge when to reef than
when on a reach or run.

Ropes don't hum when they're happy.
Judge stresses, what a line can take, whether it will
stretch before parting or go off like a cracker.
Once over-loaded, synthetic ropes become unreliable.

Like true love, a half-hitch on a cleat can be forever.
Low-friction plastic cleats and synthetic ropes may make
a final half-hitch over the horn necessary but beware,
without a full turn and several fig-of-eights a rope will 'render'
and then that hitch will seize up tight.

Mainsail - up slow and down fast.
Hoist and set with care while ensuring
that it can be dropped in a hurry.
A plug of greasy rag riding on a spare sail slide,
with a downhaul, will keep the track lubricated.
Grooves are all-up or all-out systems,
they don't encourage a quick drop.

**Don't follow fishing boats
unless you want to pick cockles**.
In short, if you're hoping to learn a new route DON'T.
In fact don't follow any strange boat unless you know
her draught and intention.

The test of a knot is untying it.
A correctly made knot, bend, or hitch can always be untied.
Other incorrect ones may hold securely but they'll hold for life!

Right-of-way may mean sail over power.
Don't bank on it!

Never push your luck - the big ship may be unable
or unwilling to alter:
Fred was right as he sailed along
Now he's as dead as if he was wrong.

Don't berth in a fishing port
and expect to be treated as a yacht.

Fishermen come and go at all hours and in all states of sobriety.
They have no reverence for topsides.
They are earning their livings, how about you?

**The way to find the isolated rock
is to leave it to your auto-pilot.**
Or a solitary angler's dinghy, unlit buoy, sewer outfall beacon.
It is all too easy to credit an auto with intelligence.
Take full 360 degree scans between dives below.
It can't see and it wouldn't tell you even if it could .

**A fender in hand is worth
two on the wrong side.**
Tricky berthing!
The skipper has gone falsetto,
can't decide which side to berth.
Hang a fender on each beam,
hold one in reserve and keep
your head down.

Fat sailors and headlands need wide berths.
In bad weather at night, making for the shelter of a headland,
never clip close to the point; there may be off-lying rocks
and dangerous tidal over-falls or rips where seas break heavily.
Swing wide, stay safe.

Don't relax until anchored or moored.
The sight of shelter ahead lures us into relaxing vigilance
- that is when engines stall, dinghies shoot out
under our bows and men in peaked caps
start hollering from the harbour office.

Drat the sailor who looks aloft but rarely goes there.
Only regular, personal inspection of mast and fittings
can bring peace of mind on a wild night.
Crosstrees get damaged alongside in marinas.

Don't point your bows at it if the ship don't go there.

(Fisherman's maxim.)

Pinching simply results in stalling the sails,

especially in a sea-way.

Result: excessive leeway for minimum headway.

Sail full-and-by, i.e. by the wind but

with sails full and driving.

**Motor-sailing;
push her too hard
and she'll dig a hole and
wallow in it.**
Every vessel has an optimum
hull-speed; pushing above
it builds up large bow and
quarter waves with a deep
trough between - once you
see this happening ease her
and watch the speed.

Let her waltz with the waves.
On a long offshore beat, settle the sheets a fraction,
bear off and steer easy - let her sidle through the waves
instead of bashing through them.
Losing a degree to leeward is only one mile in sixty
- an extra short leg on arrival.

A roll in the main is worth an extra half-knot.
Maybe more. Once she's pinned down and
staggering she makes leeway and the increased
use of rudder slows her still further.
A night-watchman's hut sails better.
Learn how far you can press her.

Jib rolled too small,
no use at all.

Roller headsails are a boon
- until it blows. Rolling small
raises the Centre of Effort,
destroys shape and increases
sheet length
- which defies flattening in.
Most people just motor.
Rig a movable stay and small jib.

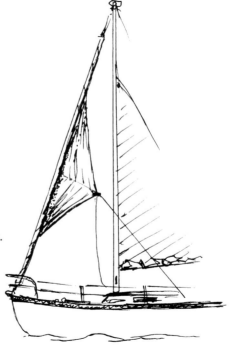

Reverse with panache, CRASH!
Reverse too soon, miss the pontoon.
Berthing flat out then going full astern is the hallmark
of jack-the-lad, a recipe for disaster.
Ideally keep full steerage way.
Going astern too hard will spin her stern
which may be either helpful or ruinous.

When drying out alongside.
Heavy list with good intent
Boat secure, stanchions bent,
Slight list stanchions fine
Let's hope you rigged a masthead line.

And when she's dried out by the wall....
Don't forget the rise and fall.
Don't forget to look aloft
Walls are hard and masts are soft.

Good seamanship is greasing seacocks.
And seizing the anchor shackle,
coiling ropes, updating charts,
stopping to eat and sleep properly,
taking nothing for granted.

Not 'Can you hang on?' as much as 'Can you let go?'

When reaching for a buoy with the boathook never hang
on at full stretch of arm, boathook and body
- you won't be able to unhook it if the skipper makes
a cock-up and sheers off. Very nasty and extremely funny.

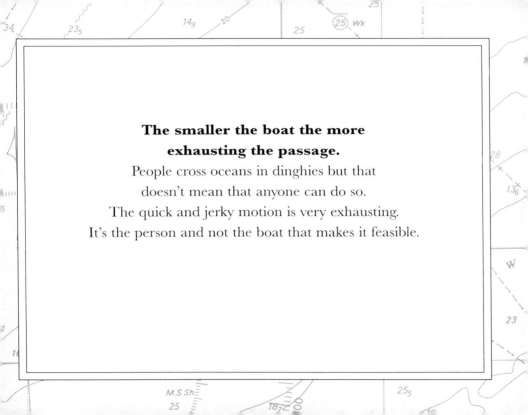

**The smaller the boat the more
exhausting the passage.**
People cross oceans in dinghies but that
doesn't mean that anyone can do so.
The quick and jerky motion is very exhausting.
It's the person and not the boat that makes it feasible.

**A line hurled in haste
is like a sinner
begging absolution.**
It falls at your feet.
Coil with care,
heave with slow deliberation -
and not at the lolly-licking
day-tripper who just
happened to be
on the quay.

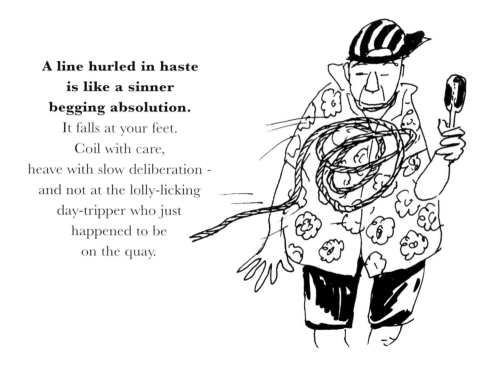

Fog is scary but a haze is sly.
Haziness can conceal the deterioration of
visibility, 200 metres looks no different to
half a mile, ships creep up unseen.
How long do buoys remain visible astern?
Drop a balled-up newspaper, time it out of sight.

Fitting out just for the passage is like dispensing with your spare tyre.

'We've never needed it before!'

You either go to sea or you don't.

The boat must be ready for anything.

You can end the shortest passage with

a rescuer's blanket round your shoulders

and your picture in the paper!

The best look-out is on the helm.
The helm views all that happens on board
and around, don't obscure the view.
Classic is the forehatch left open and upright
hiding the dinghy dead ahead
- and old dad was only going ashore for fresh croissants!

Autumn boats are tired boats.

A season of hard sailing tires boats and crews alike,

but crews can rest.

Best not extend the season without a good check aloft and alow.

Grounding her for a scrub!

Classic (unconvincing) excuse.

NEVER on HW top springs - you can be stuck for a month!

Never at half-ebb when the level drops fastest .

If you must ground, do it on the flood or the last of the ebb.

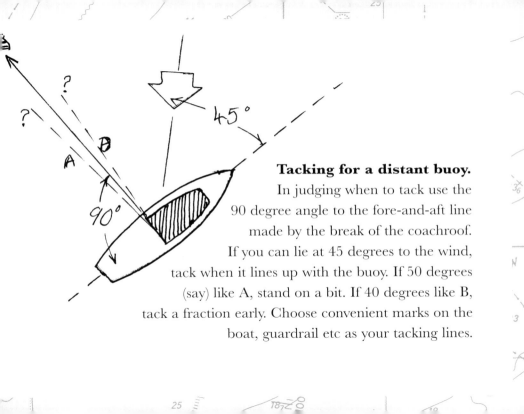

Tacking for a distant buoy.

In judging when to tack use the 90 degree angle to the fore-and-aft line made by the break of the coachroof. If you can lie at 45 degrees to the wind, tack when it lines up with the buoy. If 50 degrees (say) like A, stand on a bit. If 40 degrees like B, tack a fraction early. Choose convenient marks on the boat, guardrail etc as your tacking lines.

**Engines solve most minor problems
- minor problems are the best teachers.**
Try it under sail with the engine on tick-over in neutral,
that way you will gain confidence in boat-handling
- some day it may spare you the pain of a rescue tow and
a wigging from the Harbour Master's nark.

An afternoon sail, down-wind, is like living on credit.
And the typical reach-out-and-back can also fool you.
Speed increases, apparent wind heads you, so you bear off
a shade. The reach back becomes a hard close-hauled thrash .
A wet and shuddering girlfriend is an ominous sight.

4. Anchors and anchoring

**An anchor on the seabed is like an errant husband
- out of sight and God knows what it's up to!**

Every type of anchor, every seabed differs. Study them.

A digger on a rocky bottom or a pick in soft

mud are equally suspect on a windy night.

Which conditions are best for your anchor?

Find out, then make allowances.

Anchor buoys should be small and on a short scope.
If you don't want some muffin to mistake it for a mooring!
Short scope helps indicate where your anchor lies
and avoids fouling the prop and rudder
when raising anchor to get under way.

A kinked chain can hazard the ship.
It can jam when letting go and it weakens chain.
Turns build up in the locker throughout the season,
a rope lashing will absorb them. Also beware chain piling
up as it is hauled in - it falls over and snags.
Prior to letting go, haul up and run back to clear them.

Bitter-end or lose the lot.
The very end of the cable stowed below
MUST ALWAYS BE SECURED.
With chain especially and in deep water, once it starts to run it
goes with a roar. You may dance a merry fandango to stop it.
Nothing can.

A rumbling anchor is trying to tell us something.
It could be tide-swing or the anchor dragging.
Hold the cable outboard.
If it tightens and rises then rumbles
as it sags veer cable, wake wife.

An inch of swell - roll like hell!
Island or headland may give shelter
from wind, not from swell.
On approaching heave-to and note masts
already there, breakers on shore.
Swells are periodic, you lie quiet for
five minutes then roll like a horse.

Foul anchor, use a chain collar.

Suitable for CQR, Meon, Bruce and other stockless types.
Make a dinner-plate size chain collar, lower it down the
anchor cable from the dinghy and tow it ahead so that
it slips down over the anchor shank. Heave away.

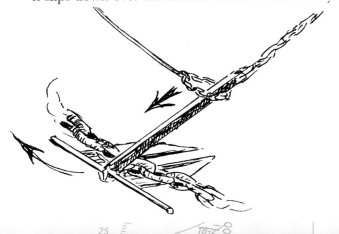

**One scope long another one short,
come 3 a.m. we'll see some sport!**
In a congested anchorage swinging circles may overlap
- fine if all have the same scope out.
Come the turn of tide there'll be a pyjama party!
Ask your nearest neighbours what cable they've got out.

While at anchor you can swing on a spring.
In a rolly anchorage you can sometimes convert a beam roll to
a more acceptable pitching by securing a line to your cable
outside the stem. Lead it aft to cock her bows athwart the swell.

On a lee shore any windshift is favourable.
It will give you a safe slant for sailing
off should your engine play up.
Even a faint onshore breeze should be eyed with deep
suspicion because it can freshen within minutes.

Chain should self-stow or you'll need someone below.
Getting under way from an open anchorage,
loose chain on deck can roar overboard as the yacht heels.
It should self-stow of its own weight, you may not
always have somebody pulling it down for you.

A swinging circle includes the backstay.
When surveying the situation include your
boat-length in your swinging circle.
Motor round twice and anchor once (but don't let some
creep nip in and bag your spot in the meantime).

A vessel isn't lost because her anchor is too big.
For peace of mind choose the largest anchor which you
can handle comfortably, whatever the pundits tell you.
Quiet nights are worth a few grunts.

Weedy seabed, worried skipper.

Kelp, pipeweed etc builds a mat under your anchor.
The danger is that it may seem to be holding, then the wind
freshens..... In clear water tell-tale dark patches warn you,
in murky waters go full astern, bang it in hard.

Mud is the beginner's best friend.

Errors of judgement when anchoring in muddy creeks
rarely result in worse than a few blushes.
Be prepared to get very, very mucky.

Cliffs grow in the dark.
They merge with their reflection.
You'll let go half a mile offshore.

Crossed cables, cross skippers.
It is always the other skipper's fault
and it can lead to much howling.
Bring your boat alongside the other (or whichever is the larger).
Pass your cable to remove the cross at your leisure.
Watch your crosstrees!

Kedge warp; pay out from dinghy not deck.
When laying off a kedge, if the warp runs from the yacht
it will have to be towed through the water;
from the dinghy it will be laid as you go.
Flake, not coil it down on the bottom of the dinghy.

Headlands in fluky winds offer uncertain shelter.
An unsteady wind can make a point or headland
a shelter or a lee shore in a single shift.
Keep an anchor watch or the first stunning crash will be
the only intimation of trouble - putting it mildly!

Moor fore-and-aft, let her swing.

Mooring between kedge and bower in a fresh beam wind
invites both to drag. Secure kedge to bower cable, pay out
a bit of slack in the latter. She can now swing bow-to-wind.

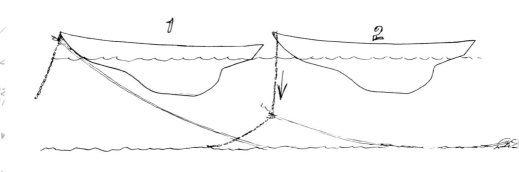

A sheering ship makes a poor neighbour.

Drop your kedge under-foot
(ie directly under the boat)
to drag to and fro, or bend

a length of heavy chain to
your cable at half-scope.

Beware the only free gap left in the anchorage.

Like the last prize in the raffle, there's probably
something dubious about it - foul seabed,
busy harbour ferry route, coaster's turning space.
Go canny. Of course you just might be incredibly lucky!
Want to bet?

Anchor scope, three for chain five for rope.

E.g max depth x 3 or 5. These are minimums.
Factors such as wind, sea, tide,
yacht windage must be considered.
Be prepared to veer 6x or 10x. Carry enough cable.

Sleeping anchor sleeping ship.
Conversely a restless anchor should mean an alert crew.
Wind-against-tide conditions keep you on your toes.
Once the tide turns and she lies quiet,
veer another few metres and crash out.

Freshen the nip (alter length).
Lying to a buoy, plunging in a gale, double back
your best warp to lie a length or more to leeward.
This means you can slip in an emergency.
Keep 'freshening the nip' so that chafe
at buoy and fairlead are altered.

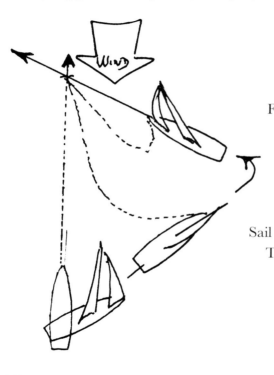

Sailing the anchor out.

Fun - maybe for real one day.
Hoist sail and back the jib
- ease the mainsheet a fraction.
Let her sail closehauled
until the anchor cable
is growing taut, then tack.
Sail along the cable hauling in fast.
Take a turn and HANG ON!

Sheer towards the shallows on the flood.

If you're forced to anchor too close to river
edge shallows, lash the helm so that she sheers
towards them throughout the flood stream;
if she nudges them it's no problem,
she'll sheer out towards deep water on the ebb.

Kedge-laying in mud - double the usual scope.

You may drag half of it home before the anchor bites.

Dragging alarm - to wake the dead!

Drop the dinghy anchor under-foot on a light line, hitched to a pile of pans. If the ship drags the line tightens 'clang, bang crash'.

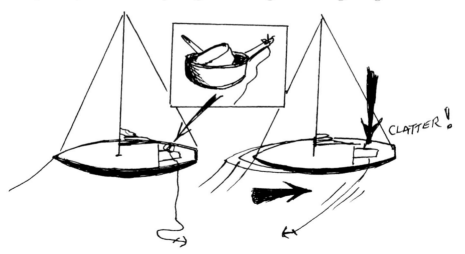

CLATTER!

Anchor foul, heavy crew works for you.

All hands to the bows, anchor taut up-and-down.

Secure it and all run aft.

If that won't work try the chain collar mentioned earlier.

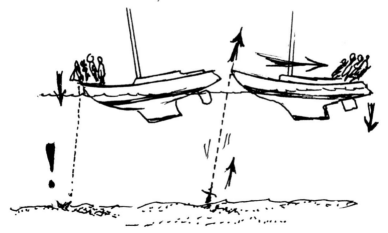

Temporary anchorage take no risks.

If the seabed is suspected to be foul, 'skow' the anchor.
Secure the rode to the crown or fluke end and then lash lightly
at the shackle. Keep a watch. If the anchor
fouls, get all hands foreward, haul taut,
all run aft to snap the lashing - the anchor
can then be pulled out backwards.

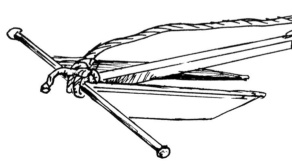

A dinghy anchor is not a kedge.
Kedges and urgency frequently go together:
choose one only slightly smaller than your main anchor.

5. Pilotage and navigation

A 3-point fix is like a camp stool - spread the legs wide.
Bearings should be evenly and well spaced. Identify any dodgy-looking ones. A suspect bearing can, accidentally, produce a dangerously neat cocked hat. In rough conditions repeat all bearings at least twice.

Following your leaders.

Entering a river on leading marks or lights, 'push' the rear
or back marks port or starboard with the upper wheel spoke.
In the case of tiller steering 'push' the front mark.
Check compass course made against the chart.

Read the chart and read the water.

Especially in shoal waters or with fast currents.
Note up-wellings, smooth slicks,
overfalls betraying submerged ledges.
Channels through shallows are marked by smooths
or ripples, indicating wind with or against current.

'Ware wishful thinking.

The more anxious you are to find a distant mark,
the greater the chance of imagining it - any that appear
in the right place and at the right time will do.
Healthy cynicism can save a deal of sorrow.

The finest of electronic navigators all lack one button.

The one marked 'hoss-sense'.
Never renounce your ability to reason.
A blind acceptance of position means that
you never doubt anything that plugs in,
whether it looks right or wrong.

Never dismiss a hunch - examine it.
Hunches are often the prodding of the subconscious mind
and long-stored knowledge, an ancient instinct gone rusty.
An uneasy feeling may be a warning to be heeded
- or just indigestion.

The compass may be hypnotic - sleeeeep!
On a very dark night the lighted compass bowl
can mesmerise the helmsman and despite wind,
rain and general grot induce sleep.
Fit a rheostat so that you can dim it.
A too-bright compass also ruins night vision.

Sea-sick navigators hit things. Eat right.
It wasn't the rock that wrecked him
There's little doubt about that,
Unless I'm mistaken
It was the sausage and bacon
And the fried bread dripping with fat!

**The more powerful the binocular,
the steadier the hand must be.**
In a small yacht high magnification glasses are a waste.
An '8x' magnification is all you can use in a bit of a chop.
Go for a zoom lens or a second instrument. If you must.

Cross the bar before you reach it.
Find an exact position nearby and take a sounding,
compare with the depth on the chart,
anything over it can be applied to the bar.
Beware signs of breakers;
seen from seaward, waves look smaller.

The shore always looks closer than it is.
Study human figures: at 600 metres they are featureless dashes,
at 400 a walker's moving legs are visible,
at 120 mouths and eyes appear as dots,
faces are recognizable at 80 metres.
('Oh my God it's your wife!')

**You've never got your stop-watch
when the light appears.**
With a bit of practice you can time it by saying;
'I-reckon-that's-ONE I-reckon-that's TWO etc.
If you're in a bit of a flap you'll count faster.

Being proved wrong is good for a navigator's soul.
When you have proved beyond all mathematical
doubt that you are in the channel,
the ensuing thump is a tonic for all on board.

On small scale charts rocks appear as dots.

Lacking a large scale chart don't try short-cuts.
Rocks are mere specks and often obscured by print.
Not even a magnifying glass justifies a needless risk.
Go somewhere else, there's always a choice.

The smoother the sea, the nicer the navigation, the neater the chart.

Conversely the rougher the going the rougher the navigation -
which is a fat lot of comfort with a 2 metre shoal ahead.
Avoid complex navigation.
If necessary heave-to and concentrate, don't go hell-for-leather.

**GPS tells us where we are,
if we're seasick we don't give a damn.**
Call it 'factor X'.
The ultimate safety of all on board may
come down to a dodgy bit of fish pie.
If you find that you really can't cope,
alter course for open water and call for help.

**If at three hours ebb she sticks,
you may be there another six.**

Sea level drops (and rises) fastest at half-tide.
If you ground at half-flood you'll be off in
a matter of moments but if you ground
at half-ebb you may have to wait until
the next 2-3 hours of new flood to get off.

Navigating a channel with a fast tide under you, plot beam bearings last.

Beam bearings alter fast and most, fore-and-aft angles alter least and more slowly. Take and plot them first then take and plot the fast-changing beam bearings second and last for an up-to-the-moment position.

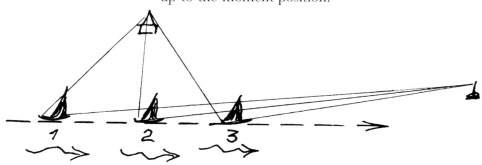

**Don't assume anything, check it,
especially when keen to get in.**
This is when distant garage forecourt lights can look
like a longed-for harbour entrance fixed red,
or when a 'church tower conspic' (one of half a dozen)
can be made to fit the picture.
Take a bearing.

'Ware the crew with 'local knowledge'.
This expert may have secret doubts but pride precludes
a baring of the breast! The skipper holds final responsibility
- not the pilot. Keep your plot going.

6. Cruise and passage planning

Cruising means freedom to change your mind.
Unlike a race or a commercial voyage, we cruise solely
for the pleasure of getting almost anywhere.
Why be boot-faced and steely-grey and bash
our crews half-witless just to reach some upwind
destination that nobody wants anyway?

**Cruising with small children:
never mind the scenery
where's the sand?**

Kids have a low boredom threshold en route.
One hour per year of age up to five is about the limit
- and 'Mummy that wretched teddy's been sick again!'

Make them a distraction to pass the time.

Whittle a toy submarine one foot long, ballast it to give negative buoyancy, fit copper diving vanes and tow it. It planes when towed short, dives if tugged.

Harness the kids
and leave 'em to it.

**The more-ports-in-fewer-days policy
is like gulping a fine liquer.**
Designate port C as the limit,
if you then make port D it will be a bonus.
But if you make for port D first
and fail to reach it - disappointment.

Stride out, tip-toe back.
If the weather is settled, making straight for your ultimate
destination in one or two long legs and then cruising
slowly home in day hops means that should the weather turn
grotty you will get home without strain.

Don't spring a surprise night passage on them.
Skippers who brood all day, then announce a night passage
just as people are trudging back from beach or sight-seeing
deserve to be hammered into the ground like a tent peg!
Remember, they are on holiday!

Night passages are best started in daylight.
Body-clocks are not yet howling for sleep,
eyes can get accustomed to the dark slowly,
work on deck is easier.

Winter nights are two days long.

Passage-making in winter is not for the faint-hearted,
nights are about fourteen hours long
and the cold penetrates the thickest clothing.
Work to short watches and keep the Bovril coming.

Headlands are the Viking's signposts.

Headlands have always been navigational aids
- they are also the greatest ship-killers.
Every headland has many different profiles according to
the angle from which it's viewed, light and shadow etc.
From close inshore false headlands
can appear as the coastline bulges.

Halfway there or halfway back?
The 'point of no return' is nothing of the sort.
In deteriorating weather and no sure idea where the hell
you are going to find shelter ahead, it may make more
sense to go back to the harbour you know better.

You don't stop to tie your laces in the fast lane.
Cross shipping lanes fast and square to the traffic.
You may have to shave past the stern of one ship
in order to cross the bows of the next safely
- it's the one after that you need to worry about.

The yacht can take it if the crew can.
With a hard passage in prospect you check sails, gear
and stowages. Consider how many of the crew will stay the
course, whether shelter can be reached en route? Is it on?
Harbour decisions lack reality.

Don't explore on the peak of top springs.
If you don't know the waters it's best to bring up
at anchor for the few hours around high water.
Grounding means being 'neaped'
- part of the scenery for the next fortnight or more.

Compasses and friends - trust both almost completely.
You should be able to trust your compass but only by being
alert to the possibility of damage or deviation.
Check while sailing whenever transits,
buoy-to-buoy lines and shore marks offer the opportunity.

God makes Variation, Man makes deviation.
Don't hire an expensive compass adjuster and stow
an outboard motor in an adjacent cockpit locker.

Gremlins in the cockpit.
Using a bearing compass, stand amidships in the companionway.
Check that there are no electrics up under the coachroof.

Taking a set of bearings is a special skill.
Don't dwell too long, try for a steady sweep
calling out the bearings to an
assistant, go round a couple of times.
This is how motor torpedo boat navigators did it.

Headlands are tidal gates.
The temptation is to catch a tide fair at a headland and
motor-sail like a bat out of hell to make it at the next.
The ultimate result is a hurried cruise and a sense of irritation
if you miss a tide. Gear down, cruise don't race.

**On passage relax, sail at a pace
that doesn't exhaust the crew.**
Heave-to as a matter of routine.
Heave-to for a leisurely supper, to sort out the navigation,
top up the tank, wait offshore for a lock to open.
Until you have tried it you don't realise
how much it relieves the pressure.

Ships in shipping lanes often bunch up.

If you see a procession of ships athwart your course,
it often pays to slow down or heave-to until they pass
- there is often a clear spell to come.

Don't try to steer a long down-wind leg
with novices on the helm.

Steer two long quartering legs, a zig and a zag.
A dead run will be nerve-racking for all.
Be prepared for the course made good to be
to windward of the course ordered.

7. Safer sailing

**An obsession with safety
makes for a gloomy shipmate.**
A safe driver can still be a cheerful companion.
Note the dangers, prepare for them then pipe down about them.
Nervous members of crew can become touchy.
Sailing suddenly ceases to be fun.

**Driving home on Sunday night
- the most dangerous time.**
The driver is tired, burning from wind and sun,
longing for bed with eyelids like manhole covers.
If you can't get some kip in, make it the passengers
serious duty to keep talking.
Once they nod off the danger becomes grave.

A coaster at 3 a.m. is the ship to watch.
She may be swinging along on auto with the
watch in the galley brewing up a pint of tea.
Never, never assume that she'll avoid you,
whatever the legal rights or wrongs.

Rain squalls in shipping lanes - vanishing ships.
Monitor visible ships constantly; ships can vanish.
Isolated heavy rain squalls miles away can
wipe out all trace of a ship's nav lights.
Suddenly she's on top of you.

The dangerous triangle - the foredeck.

When going right forward the gap in handholds between mast or shrouds and the bow pulpit tempts us to take it at the trot .
At sea rig a taut line from mast to foot of forestay.
The step down from coachroof to side deck and the first step out of the cockpit are also danger spots. Hook up.

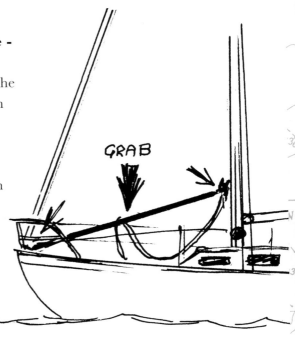

GRAB

Don't all have the moules mariniere.
When dining ashore in that little place off the tourist
rat-run, don't all order the same grub.
It just needs one dodgy bowl of shellfish to decimate
a whole crew. 'Garcon, bread-and-milk por le Capitain, ok?'

Think what a Coroner's verdict might be.
When faced with a difficult and dangerous entrance:
'Did you know the waters beyond risk of error?
Was it really essential to attempt it?
Was a promised visit to the Cafe de Port
really justification for risking your necks?'

Monday mornings keep the lifeboats busy.
Getting back in time for work prompts hundreds of crews
to dash for home when it is blowing a hoolie.
In troubled weather stay home and the hell with duty-free.

**Three feet of polythene can turn an afternoon
sail into an all-night battle.**
It takes little to clog the prop, then a rising offshore breeze
and a foul tide does the rest. Carry a very long kedge warp
and make sure that you can reef both sails efficiently.
Always carry spare grub and water.

A radar reflector isn't a four-leaf-clover.
Neither will a 'lucky Joan the Wad' guarantee being 'seen'.
A big ship may be scanning on long range,
her officers preoccupied, there may be
wave-clutter to obscure your signal.
The *****'s may not even be looking!

A sticking drawer, a wobbly table an angry navigator.
Angry navigators make mistakes.
Hunt out and remedy every tiny cause of irritation
- the door hook that rattles, the screw head that rips pockets.
Tired people are easily riled, tempers fray, mistakes are made.

An eye for trouble isn't pessimism, it's imagination.
Imagination means that you look for trouble
before it comes looking for you.
Well, what would you do if you hit
a submerged container at night?

Don't be the bacon in the butty.
Ships on potential collision courses are closing at 40-50 knots.
If you decide that you can just nip across
they won't even see you! Slow, slow let 'em go.
That way you live to bore the pants off listeners at the club bar.

When the thunder cloud shows it's slip - reef fast.
Or drop sail and hit the starter because the white base
is a squall and it could reach (briefly) storm force.
It could miss you or dismast you.

Don't ignore hull-down ships.
They are the ones you'll be dealing with in 5-10 minutes time.
They may also alter course to clear ships far ahead or for
a route alteration. Regard them as not having seen you.

A white yacht in a sunny haze is like
a white cat in a snowstorm.
You may be invisible to the lookout.
Call up on VHF. If the sun is angled right,
flash her with a mirror
- your radar reflector is a bonus.

Alter course early and boldly.
Shaping to avoid a ship, do so unmistakably.
Five degrees may clear her but
make it ten and she'll see that it will.
Also every ship is a potential run-down
if you can't see her sternlight.

In emergencies nervous sailors start their engines.

Which may be the worst thing they can do,
e.g. dismasting means ropes in the water,
man-overboard means legs at risk.
If you do start it to recover him, having got him
don't just hit neutral, switch off altogether.

How fast can you clear away the guardrail?

In a case of man-overboard and recovery, getting him aboard
will be grossly hindered by the guardrail and name dodger.
Fit a quick-release link and practise dropping it regularly.

Jumbo-size sailors - think before you jump overboard.
Or dive. Can you get back aboard? The struggle may be too much.
Overboard swimming parties
are fun but rig the boarding
ladder or inflate the dink
alongside first.
Check water temperature !

**The shroud may be a handy hand-hold
- it's strong enough. Is your grip?**

No way. Ok for a steadying hold but if your whole
body weight is involved your grip will certainly fail.

**Men who have a crafty pee overboard at night!
Never, NEVER in rough weather.**

Fundamental but serious, many, many do it
and many have gone overboard.

**In a boat where father is skipper and crew,
he can't afford to go sick.**

If you are wife-mate-novice, master the VHF,
learn to roll up the jib, start
the engine and plot a course.

It'll last another season!

I see no reason why it won't last the season
Provided we limit the strain
Well just you wait
'Till it's blowing force eight
At 3 a.m. and ******* with rain.

**The cat is in the cattery,
the milk and papers are cancelled.**
You still don't have to sail if the weather is dodgy.
Inviting friends for the weekend is another form of pressure.
Be single-minded. This is when the crew can
show solidarity in supporting the skipper.

**In bad weather the simplest tasks
become complex problems.**
Tools shoot everywhere, things get lost, tempers get frayed.
Plan for it, spread a wet towel to work on,
stow carefully so that you know where everything is,
carry two pairs of pliers - you'll lose one.

Don't dash for shelter.

Head for shelter under control. Going hell-bent with flogging sails and roaring engine leaves no latitude for the unexpected. Snug her down all round and then motor if necessary.

What's the difference between a safety harness and a frilly nightie?

None whatsoever if you don't hook on.

Skippers note: as soon as people don a harness they feel safe! Nag them until they HOOK ON.

**Guardrails are strong enough and
just high enough to trip you.**
Imagine they're not there. They are a second chance.
Don't hook on to them or you'll end up
towing alongside like a rubber duck.

Distress calls don't mean we stop trying.
Apathy is a killer.
Do something.
Get loose ropes out of the water, fire recognition
flares or show lights, wave towels, get everyone
into lifejackets, dish out comforts, stream dinghy
or raft astern, pack bag of vital belongings.

**Falling overboard at five knots means
you're forty feet astern in five seconds.**
How long does it take a shocked
helmsman to chuck a lifebuoy? Try it.
Unless you are fully under control it is better to gybe,
sail back close and place it in his hands thus buying
precious time to manoeuvre carefully.

Whatever you do keep him in view.
The basic drill of appointing an undeviating look-out
is easily forgotten in the general panic.
It is more important than anything initially.
In breaking water a head and shoulders
are hidden nine tenths of the time.

Shorten your harness line while working.

Keep it long for moving around but if using both hands to work either hitch it short or make a marline-spike hitch plus half-hitch - easily untied.

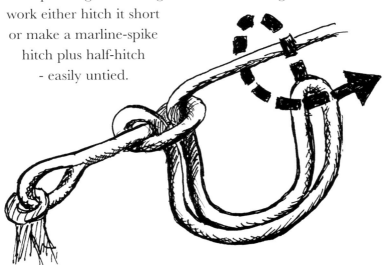

**In the bos'un's chair;
it takes strength
to get you up,
skill to get you down.**
You may be winched up like
a monkey on a stick quite safely,
lowering however means
slackening the turns first.
A turn can jump the barrel!
The lowerer must 'surge' the turns.
Left hand flat, fingers extended,
applies pressure while the right
hand eases the strain under control.

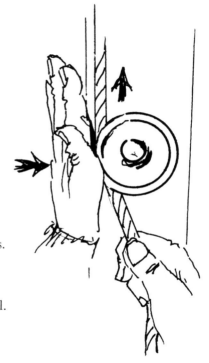

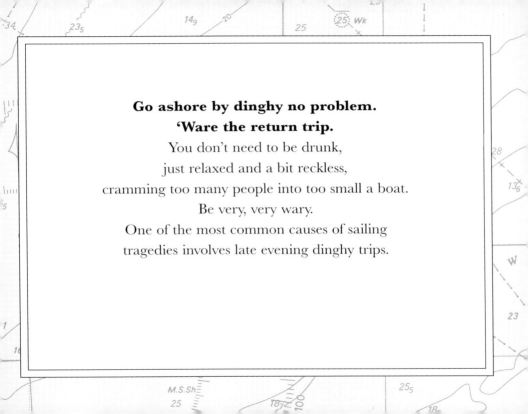

Go ashore by dinghy no problem.
'Ware the return trip.
You don't need to be drunk,
just relaxed and a bit reckless,
cramming too many people into too small a boat.
Be very, very wary.
One of the most common causes of sailing
tragedies involves late evening dinghy trips.

Don't make a wild grab for a running chain or warp.
If close to fairlead or cleat. It is all too easy for your
fingers to become trapped and seriously damaged.
Grab a turn some distance away or let it go.

Big ships look omnipotent.
The sorry truth is that the man in charge
may be a pip-squeak with a hangover,
a blinding headache and a battered love-life.
Go round his stern.

The best bilge-pump is a panicking man with a bucket.
In fibreglass boats pumps get little use.
Suppose (just to whip the smile off your face) you hit a container?
How long could you keep
pumping, how much does
your pump shift?
There's a thought
to cheer you up.

8. Wave, wind and weather

Listening to shipping forecasts is like reading a book - one page won't tell you the story.
You should start several days at least before sailing in order to get into the swing of the weather pattern. That way you can watch the development and deterioration of fronts and highs.

A barometer isn't just an ornament to polish.
Like a sheepdog, it works best for one master.
Once everybody starts pecking and rubbing
away you can't tell what it is doing.
Let the skipper tap gently three or four times a day
- and polish it too!

**Sudden movements fall or rise
are a warning to the wise.**
- Which is why only one person
should touch the barometer.
The behaviour is what you must note.
Cornish fishermen used a small-necked
bottle of water stuck in a jam-jar
- changes in barometric pressure
caused a rise and fall in the neck.
Glass jumps - stand to yer pumps.

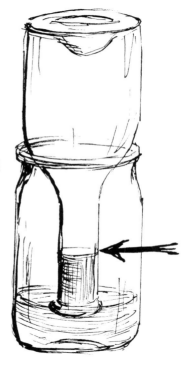

Is it a gale?

Force ten gales may be forecast, you get a good
hiding and assume that you've survived one.
Next time you treat a forecast
of force eight with indifference.
Force six and a weather-going tide is gale enough.

A swell is a wave with it's teeth out.

It may be due to a distant storm which might or might
not be heading your way. When a swell is present the
wind has only to rise and blow for a couple of hours
and you'll have a nasty old sea to cope with.

The way to win yachting friends is to make a social call at two minutes to shipping forecast time.
So tape record it. Always record it. The brain has a way of gelling out the moment a forecast begins, the milk boils over, the baby howls and somebody says 'one lump or two?'

Weather windows can slam down on your knuckles.
Quick passage; how long have we got?
The movement of a low is described as follows.
Slowly: 0-15 knots. Steadily: 15-25.
Rather quickly: 25-35. Rapidly: 35-45.
Very rapidly: over 45 knots.
Where is it centred relative to you?

Cold wind - weighty wind.

'Cold winds knocks yer dahn mate' said coasting barge skippers, who should know. Some experts (who have never flogged round Orfordness in a January gale with newspaper stuffed up their jumpers) refute this.

Clouds like cauliflowers - squally showers.

And a chance of a thunderstorm if clouds rise high like towers.
They usually follow the land,
which is meagre comfort for coasting yachts.
Keep a wary eye, unstable conditions can pack some surprises.

There's wind about, the sun is setting up his backstays.

When bars of sunlight slant down to the sea from the belly
of a large black cloud it is a sure sign of wind in the offing.
Just how much is anyone's guess but I'd as soon
be swinging to an anchor in harbour.

Rain before wind, blow not far behind.
Lousy verse but worth heeding.
First the misty murk, then a spatter of rain in the first squall,
which is the time to reef. Squalls become ever more frequent
until it is a continuous blast - and there's fun for you.

**When cats-paws spread, join and meet,
set your topsail, trim the sheet.**
After calm one of the joys of those who sail is that
first stirring of sails and the tinkle of the bow-wave.
Morning calms seldom last long.

Upper cloud contrary to the lower
- the direction to come.

Worth noting when setting forth. By tomorrow you may
have a beat on your hands - or a spinnaker run.
Likewise 'bawlies', tatters of fast-moving cloud at low level,
usually herald a stiff breeze within an hour or so.

Backing wind and falling glass,
soundly sleeps the silly ass.

Or anybody who hasn't heard a forecast, looked at the
barometer or heeded the wind direction - one heck of a lot
of cloth-eared owners who think sense is an optional extra!

**Halos belong
to the unholy.**
A halo around the sun
after fine weather:
a change for the worst,
the larger the sooner.
A halo round the moon:
also change.
Usually bad.

Sunset pale and white, you're in for a windy night.
Wet anyway. If the dawn is high (heavy cloud on the horizon)
the wind will probably be high as well.
Whether to sail, not weather for sailing
- to make an atrocious pun of it.

Same theme:
High cirrus then a halo'd sun, for shelter run.
It gets so that you dare not part the bedroom curtains
in the morning! Or tap the barometer.
'Quick rise after low, expect a stronger blow!'
'Wind backs agin the sun, trust it not for back twill run.'
Who's for tennis?

Lanes of silence.
In fog sound waves can leap-frog, a nearby sound being
inaudible but heard ten miles away and vice versa.
You can isolate by rolling a chart into a cone as an ear-trumpet.
Don't trust it, sound-waves can also bend!

Big swell, no wind, bad weather can't be far behind.
Distant disturbance heading your way (perhaps).
When the breeze begins to fill in face it and stick your right
hand out to find where the depression is centred
(northern hemisphere).

Artist's sky, sailor's warning.
In other words a highly-coloured sky and clouds with hard,
sculptured shapes make a super jig-saw puzzle picture
but herald a nasty night.

Gale force:
Wave crests blow in streaks of foam, make for home.
Long, lacy streamers fly in advance of crests,
which blow off to leeward.
In wind-against-current situations
a bad, bad sea can develop.

An inch of mercury, a foot of tide.
If tide height is important, barometric pressure can affect it.
One inch rise of mercury
(or equivalent in millibars) equals a foot of fall.
Hence a plunging barometer means
trouble for boats moored in mud berths.

A west wind shoves, a nor-west wind punches.
Nor-westerly winds associated with the cold fronts
of a passing low are often hard and squally,
typically colours are harsh and vivid.
On occasions a nor-wester can pack one hell of a punch
despite a rising glass.

**Scattered clouds, dodgy wind,
clearing sky, steady wind.**
A messy-looking sky is often a rag-bag of remnants
from broken-up bad weather clouds.
No problem with glass rising slowly.

Wind in the east, ten days at least.
Anyone who has tried to work up-Channel in
easterly weather knows this full well, hence
'the wind from the east the wind I like least'.

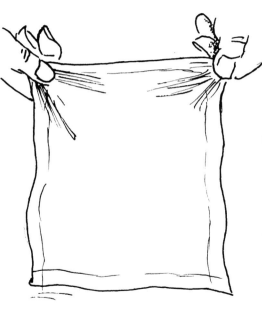

Wind speed by handkerchief.

A handkerchief held up like a flag gives a rough idea of wind speed: In Force 2 it extends lazily and almost flaps. F3, a measured flogging, beats can be counted. F 3-4 beats can't be counted. F 4 rapid, audible beat. F 5 whole area beating and continuous crackle. F 6-7 hard to hold, occasional loud whip-cracks.

Sheltering in the lee - not all it's cracked up to be.
A sheer cliff casts a sheltering wind-shadow for a distance
of cliff height x 30. A slope of the same height may
give no real shelter and winds sweep down with velocity
- even more strongly via gullies and valleys .

When waves break.
As water shallows, waves draw closer together.
Once the depth becomes less than the distance between
crests, waves become unstable and crash.
Outcrops of rock and sandbanks topple waves.
Distinguish between wind-driven crests and shoaling crests.

Wave height in open water.

The wind speed in mph divided by 2.

(For example, wind speed 20 mph, wave height 10 feet.)

Only if well offshore and uninfluenced

by land or seabed changes etc.

Tap the glass whenever you pass? Certainly NOT!

Read it every three hours.

If it falls .06 inches a storm is impending.

If .15 a strong storm, if .30 inches find a cozy cellar,

an extreme storm is coming.

To convert to millibars: pressure in inches x 33.86.

**Morning fog in the river have no fear,
by noon it should start to clear.**
Radiation mist - the cooling of moist air
- hangs in river valleys but seldom
extends more than 2-3 miles offshore.
So the cautious mariner may bumble around all day not
knowing that a few miles offshore all is clear!

**If the sky is overcast and greasy
Stay home and take it easy.**
There's wind about. But overcast and watery means rain.

Gales sneak up on you.

A gloomy drizzle and a succession of wet squalls, each a bit stronger than the preceding one. A gale is noisy, mind-numbing, demoralising and tiring. Yet maybe only one yacht in twenty can be reefed down small and efficiently enough. A truly tiny sail area is all it takes to relieve the stress.

Captain Lecky's lore.

Dirty days hath September, April, June and November. From January to May it raineth every day, all the rest hath thirty-one without a bloody gleam of sun and if any of them had two and thirty they'd be just as wet and twice as dirty. Who's arguing!

For a free, full-colour brochure write, phone or fax us:

Fernhurst Books
Duke's Path, High Street, Arundel,
West Sussex BN18 9AJ, UK.

Tel: 01903 882277
Fax: 01903 882715
Email: sales@fernhurstbooks.co.uk
Website: www.fernhurstbooks.co.uk